MICHIGAN

Past and Present

Janey Levy

rosen publishing's
rosen central®

New York

Published in 2010 by The Rosen Publishing Group, Inc.
29 East 21st Street, New York, NY 10010

Library of Congress Cataloging-in-Publication Data

Levy, Janey.
Michigan: past and present / Janey Levy.—1st ed.
    p. cm.—(The United States: past and present)
Includes bibliographical references and index.
ISBN 978-1-4358-3523-8 (library binding)
ISBN 978-1-4358-8496-0 (pbk)
ISBN 978-1-4358-8497-7 (6 pack)
1. Michigan—Juvenile literature. I. Title.
F566.3.L48 2010
977.4—dc22

                                                                    2009028025

Manufactured in the United States of America

CPSIA Compliance Information: Batch #LW10YA: For Further Information contact Rosen Publishing, New York, New York at 1-800-237-9932

On the cover: Top left: This painting by Seth Eastman shows Fort Mackinac in 1872. Top right: Rivard Plaza on the Detroit riverfront opened in June 2007 and quickly became popular with locals and visitors alike. Bottom: Sleeping Bear Dunes National Lakeshore, on the northwest coast of Michigan's Lower Peninsula, is one of the state's most famous and popular spots.

Contents

Even without the use of contrasting color, Michigan stands out on a map. No other inland state is so completely surrounded by water. This fact has shaped Michigan throughout history.

Introduction

It's easy to spot Michigan on a U.S. map. It's located on the Canadian border, surrounded by the Great Lakes, and shaped like a mitten. Two peninsulas make up the state. The Lower Peninsula (the mitten-shaped one) is the larger. The Upper Peninsula—called the U.P. by Michiganders (or Michiganians)—projects from northeastern Wisconsin, between Lakes Superior and Michigan.

The first inhabitants arrived about 11,500 years ago. Their descendants include the modern Ottawa, Chippewa (Ojibwa), and Potawatomi peoples. The state's name comes from the Chippewa word *michigama*, meaning "large lake."

Early Native Americans lived in small bands and hunted, fished, and gathered wild foods. Some also farmed. Around 1500, about one hundred thousand of them dwelled around the Great Lakes. Their lives changed forever when Europeans arrived in the 1600s.

These early people wouldn't recognize Michigan today. The population is about ten million. It's a major industrial and automobile manufacturing center, as well as an important agricultural one. It's also popular with tourists, fishermen, hunters, and filmmakers.

Many famous people—past and present—have ties to Michigan. They include great Native American leaders such as Okemos; Henry Ford, founder of the Ford Motor Company; William Keith Kellogg, the inventor of cornflakes; and modern musicians and sports figures like Stevie Wonder, Madonna, and Derek Jeter.

Chapter 1

THE LAND OF MICHIGAN

Michigan is the only state that touches four of the five Great Lakes. Lake Superior is north of the U.P. Lake Michigan, Lake Huron, and Lake Erie surround the Lower Peninsula.

The Straits of Mackinac join Lakes Michigan and Huron and separate the two peninsulas. The Mackinac Bridge, completed in 1957, spans the straits. At five miles (eight kilometers) long, it's the world's third-longest suspension bridge.

Michigan also has forty major rivers, more than thirty-five thousand lakes and ponds, and numerous wetlands.

Hundreds of islands dot Michigan's waters. More than seventy-five are named. Wolves and moose roam freely on Isle Royale. Beaver Island is called America's Emerald Isle for its lush greenery and the Irish ancestry of its inhabitants. Mackinac Island has been a popular vacation spot since the late 1800s.

The movement of glaciers during the Ice Age carved Michigan's highlands, hilly uplands, plains, and sand dunes.

The Four Regions of Michigan

Experts divide Michigan into four regional ecosystems, two in each peninsula. The Lower Peninsula has Regions I and II. Regions III

The Mackinac Bridge, seen here at sunset, presented immense construction challenges because of the stormy straits. In spite of this, it was completed in three and a half years.

and IV are in the U.P. As you might expect from the U.P.'s location, Regions III and IV are generally colder and receive more snow than Regions I and II.

Region I

Region I, the southern Lower Peninsula, has the state's highest average annual temperature and longest growing season. The landscape includes forests, prairies, moraines, low ridges, streams, rivers, ponds, lakes, and wetlands.

Like the rest of Michigan, Region I is cloudy for about half the year. Its average annual precipitation is about thirty-two inches

A Wild, Cold Land

During the Ice Age, Michigan was a much harsher place than it is today. A huge, thick ice sheet covered the state, advancing and retreating many times. Because of the ice, extreme cold, and lack of plants, animals didn't appear in Michigan until near the end of the Ice Age, when the ice sheet was making its final retreat. Familiar animals of today, such as black bears, coyotes, gray wolves, beavers, porcupines, and red squirrels, were among those that first arrived. Also included were some of the immense animals of legend: the giant beaver, flat-headed peccary, Scott's moose, woodland musk ox, mammoth, and mastodon. The giant animals couldn't survive as the climate warmed, and all are now extinct.

Although Michigan is famous for its long, cold winters, its climate isn't nearly as severe. It has mild summers that support agriculture in many parts of the state, and its numerous natural areas sustain a wide variety of wildlife. The state, especially the U.P., is popular with winter sports enthusiasts because of the great amounts of snow. The Keweenaw Peninsula, which sticks out from the northwest corner of the U.P. (and is the northernmost part of mainland Michigan), can get up to twenty-one feet (six meters) of snow per year, more than any other place in the state. Snow usually arrives in the Keweenaw Peninsula by the middle of November and stays until the end of April. The average January temperature there is about 14 degrees Fahrenheit (–10 degrees Celsius). In spite of the long, winters, lots of animals live in the Keweenaw Peninsula, including black bears, red foxes, coyotes, snowshoe hares, and flying squirrels.

A mammoth (left) and a mastodon (right) resemble elephants. Only the mammoth is related to them.

(eight-one centimeters). In July the average temperature is 72°F (22°C). In January the average temperature is 24°F (−4°C).

The plants include aspen and hardwood trees, such as maple and oak. You will also find grasses, reeds, wild-flowers, and carnivorous, or meat-eating, sundews and pitcher plants, which eat mostly insects.

The region has a rich assortment of animals. One of the strangest animals is

The painted turtle was adopted as Michigan's state reptile in 1995. Painted turtles live for decades and prefer quiet, shallow water.

the wolverine. Although believed to have vanished from the state about two hundred years ago, one was seen—and photographed—in the northern part of the "thumb" in 2004.

There are also wild turkeys, songbirds, owls, woodpeckers, eagles, hawks, and many sorts of water birds. You can see frogs, toads, sala-manders, turtles, snakes, and lizards, too.

Region II

Region II, the northern Lower Peninsula, has a cooler, more variable climate than Region I. Its landscape includes forests, grasslands, uplands, moraines, beaches, sand dunes, rivers, streams, ponds, lakes, and wetlands.

Its average annual precipitation is 30 inches (76 cm). July's aver-age temperature is 68°F (20°C), while January's is 22°F (−6°C).

Region II's plants include hardwood trees, pine, cedar, and fir. You'll also see grasses, wildflowers, and carnivorous pitcher plants.

Many animals that live in Region I are found here as well, although you might also encounter bobcats, cougars, elk, and snowshoe hares. Many of the birds, amphibians, and reptiles found in Region I reside here, too.

Region III

Region III, the eastern half of the U.P., is generally cool, with a shorter growing season than Regions I and II, and lots of lake-effect snow and rain. The landscape is mostly flat, with plains, meadows, low moraines, forests, sand dunes, beaches, rivers, lakes, and wetlands. It also has some coastal cliffs and waterfalls.

As with all of Michigan, it's very cloudy. The average annual precipitation is 33 inches (84 cm). The average July temperature is 64°F (18°C), while January's average temperature is 18°F (–8°C).

The trees include hardwood, pine, aspen, birch, spruce, and cedar. Wildflowers, including wild orchids, grow here, as do ferns and mosses.

In addition to many animals common in the northern Lower Peninsula, you can find moose and martens here. You'll also see many of the same species of birds.

Region IV

Regions I through III are surrounded by the Great Lakes, which moderate their climates. However, because the lakes don't completely surround Region IV, the western half of the U.P., they have less influence on its climate. As a result, Region IV is more like the northern plains, with long and very cold, snowy winters and short, hot summers.

It also has the most rugged landscape of all the regions. You'll find bedrock ridges scraped bare by Ice Age glaciers, moraines, plains, uplands, forests, mountains, cliffs, lakes, ponds, streams, rivers, and wetlands.

Region IV is like the other regions in one way: It's very cloudy. The average annual precipitation is 34 inches (86 cm). The average July temperature is only 66°F (19°C), while January's average temperature is a frigid 16°F (–9°C).

Tahquamenon Falls, shown here, are found in Region III and are considered among Michigan's most beautiful waterfalls.

Its widespread forests contain hardwoods, aspen, pine, spruce, and cedar. Grasses, ferns, and mosses also grow here, as do wild orchids and other wildflowers. You can find wild fruits such as plums, cherries, raspberries, and blueberries, too.

The wildlife here is similar to that of Region III, although you may also happen upon a fisher, a large, carnivorous member of the weasel family.

Chapter 2

The History of MICHIGAN

Michigan's history began about 11,500 years ago, when the ancestors of modern Native Americans arrived. Their descendants became the state's three main tribes (the Three Fires, as their league was called): the Ottawa, Chippewa, and Potawatomi. The Ottawa and Chippewa occupied parts of the U.P. and the northern Lower Peninsula. The Potawatomi occupied the southwestern Lower Peninsula.

The Ottawa were hunters, gatherers, farmers, and traders. The Chippewa were hunters and gatherers. The Potawatomi were farmers and hunters. However, the arrival of French explorers, traders, and missionaries in the early 1600s forever altered their way of life.

The French in Michigan

The French were the first Europeans to visit Michigan. Around 1620, Étienne Brûlé reached Sault Ste. Marie by canoe. More French explorers soon followed. They weren't especially interested in establishing colonies. Some were seeking the fabled Northwest Passage—a water route through North America to Asia and its riches. Others were interested in the wealth from the fur trade.

Along with the explorers and fur traders came French missionaries, who set up headquarters at Sault Ste. Marie. Father Jacques

In 1668, Father Jacques Marquette set up the mission of St. Mary in Sault Ste. Marie. This 1921 painting shows Marquette *(standing)* with Louis Joliet and their Native American guides.

Marquette—famous for his later exploration of the Mississippi River with Louis Jolliet—built a fort and chapel there in 1668.

Among the French who came for the fur trade was Antoine de la Mothe, Sieur (Lord) de Cadillac. He arrived in 1694 to command Fort de Buade, located on the U.P. at what is now St. Ignace. When the fort was closed, Cadillac convinced Count Pontchartrain, the minister in charge of France's North American ventures, that a new fort was needed. In 1701, he established Fort Pontchartrain—named in the count's honor—at what is today Detroit.

It wasn't long before the French missed the income from the U.P. fur trade and regretted closing Fort de Buade. Around 1715, they built

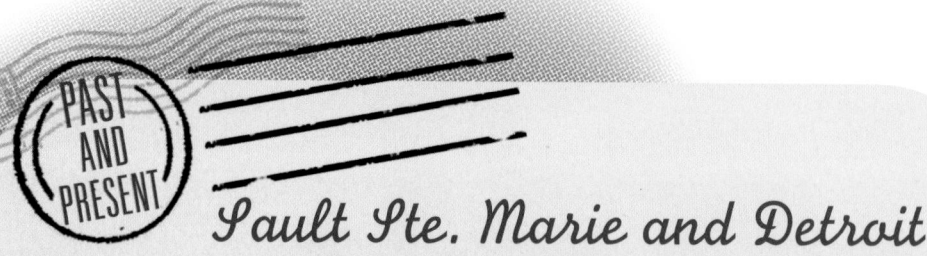

Sault Ste. Marie and Detroit

Sault Ste. Marie is Michigan's oldest European city. Long before that, however, many Native American tribes met there seasonally because of the excellent fishing and hunting. They called it the Gathering Place. French fur traders began to visit in the 1600s, and they named it Sault du Gastogne, in honor of King Louis XIII's brother. Father Jacques Marquette founded a mission there in 1668 and renamed the site Sault Ste. Marie (after Mary, the mother of Jesus). A fence 12 feet (4 m) high surrounded the small mission. Today, Sault Ste. Marie, with more than fourteen thousand people, is the U.P.'s second-largest city (after Marquette). It's also a popular tourist spot because of its history and the famous Soo Locks, which are the busiest in the world. They were built in the 1850s to allow large ships to pass around the rapids of the St. Marys River.

Detroit was founded by Antoine de la Mothe, Sieur de Cadillac, in 1701. But the area's first people were probably ancient Native Americans known as Mound Builders. Later Native American tribes, fur traders, and missionaries followed them. Cadillac chose the site to protect areas that France claimed from attacks by the British. Cadillac chose the fort's name, Fort Pontchartrain du Détroit (*détroit* means "strait"), to honor Count Pontchartrain. Today, Detroit, with nearly one million people, is far larger than any other city in Michigan. It's a struggling industrial center that's also famous for its arts, music, and sports.

About 10,000 ships pass through the Soo Locks annually.

Fort Michilimackinac on the south side of the Straits of Mackinac, at present-day Mackinaw City.

Struggles between France and England over the fur trade led to war in 1754. When the war—known as the French and Indian War—ended in 1763, the British had won and gained control of Michigan.

These houses are part of Fort Michilimackinac's village, which burned down in 1781. However, it's been rebuilt exactly as it was.

The British in Michigan

Problems quickly arose between the British and Native Americans. Because the French were mostly interested in wealth from the fur trade, they worked to establish friendships with Native Americans. They understood that the Native American gift-giving tradition helped maintain good relations between groups, and they adopted it. At first, the British promised to continue French policies. However, they didn't, and Native Americans began to understand that the British threatened their traditional way of life. In 1763, Ottawa chief Pontiac led an uprising of Ottawa, Potawatomi, and Huron warriors and tried to capture Fort Detroit. Their attempts failed.

Although Pontiac's revolt did not succeed, the British wanted to prevent similar events in the future. They tried to restore peace by issuing the Proclamation of 1763, which said colonists couldn't settle on land west of the Appalachian Mountains. Michigan became a permanent Native American territory, under the control of the British military.

The Proclamation of 1763 was just one of many British laws that angered colonists. Many believed the time had come for the colonies to become an independent nation. The American Revolution finally erupted in 1775. When it ended in 1783, the colonies became the United States of America and gained control of Michigan.

Michigan as Part of the United States

Michigan's small population of white settlers meant it could not qualify to be a state. In 1787, Congress created the Northwest Territory and made Michigan part of it. In 1800, Congress formed Indiana Territory, which included western Michigan. Five years later, Congress created Michigan Territory, which contained the areas that became Michigan, Indiana, and Illinois.

By 1833, Michigan's population was large enough for it to become a state, but its border dispute with neighboring Ohio—already a state— prevented that from happening. Meanwhile, Michigan prepared for statehood by writing its first constitution in 1835. It finally became the twenty-sixth U.S. state on January 26, 1837. The state continued to build its population by encouraging immigration, attracting mostly Germans, Canadians, Dutch, Cornish, Irish, and Scandinavians.

Tensions within the country over slavery and the Southern states' right to withdraw from the Union finally led to the Civil War in 1861. Michigan strongly opposed slavery and fought for the Union, which won the war in 1865.

Around 1900, Michigan became an important manufacturing center. In 1898, C. W. Post invented Grape-Nuts cereal, which he manufactured in Battle Creek. The city also became the site of

Kellogg's, established in 1906 by W. K. Kellogg to produce the cornflakes he had invented. Although Battle Creek became the nation's cereal capital, perhaps more significant were the events that took place in Detroit. In 1899, Ransom E. Olds moved Michigan's first automobile company, Olds Motor Vehicle Company, from Lansing to the city founded by Cadillac, and he renamed the company

This photograph from about 1922 shows factory assembly-line workers packaging Kellogg's Corn Flakes cereal.

Olds Motor Works. In 1903, Henry Ford established the Ford Motor Company there. Detroit became America's automobile manufacturing center, and its cars changed the country forever.

Beginning in the late 1900s, Detroit faced challenges from foreign automobile manufacturers, many of whom built assembly plants in other parts of the country. The economic problems that developed in 2007 also hurt the automobile industry and Michigan's economy, forcing the state's leaders to reconsider Michigan's future. The University of Michigan, founded in Ann Arbor in 1841, has become one of the nation's leading universities, and many people believe Michigan's future depends on promoting a leading role for education.

Chapter 3

THE GOVERNMENT OF MICHIGAN

In 1835, while still a territory, Michigan held a convention in Detroit to write a constitution. Voters approved the document in October 1835, and statehood followed in 1837. In 1847, the state capital was moved from Detroit to Lansing.

Like the U.S. Constitution, the Constitution of Michigan of 1835 has a bill of rights. Although the U.S. Constitution lists the rights after the document's main body, in the first ten amendments, the Michigan constitution actually began with them. It then explained who was eligible to vote, how the state government was organized, what its powers were, how to remove officials from office, how to amend the constitution, and it created a state militia and prohibited slavery.

The Michigan Constitution

A new constitution created in 1850 replaced the 1835 version. In turn, it was replaced in 1908. The current constitution was adopted in 1963 (although it has been amended numerous times since then) and is known as the Constitution of the State of Michigan of 1963.

Like the 1835 constitution, the 1963 constitution begins with a declaration of rights. It differs from the earlier one in having a much longer section on the powers, duties, and officials of local governments and a long section on finance and taxation. It provides two methods for amendment. In the first method, the state's legislature proposes an amendment. Two-thirds of the members of Michigan's senate and house of representatives must approve a proposed amendment. Then a majority of the state's voters must approve it. In the second method, the state's citizens may propose an amendment by presenting a petition signed by a number of voters equal to at least 10 percent of the number who voted for the governor in the last election. A majority of the state's voters must then approve the amendment.

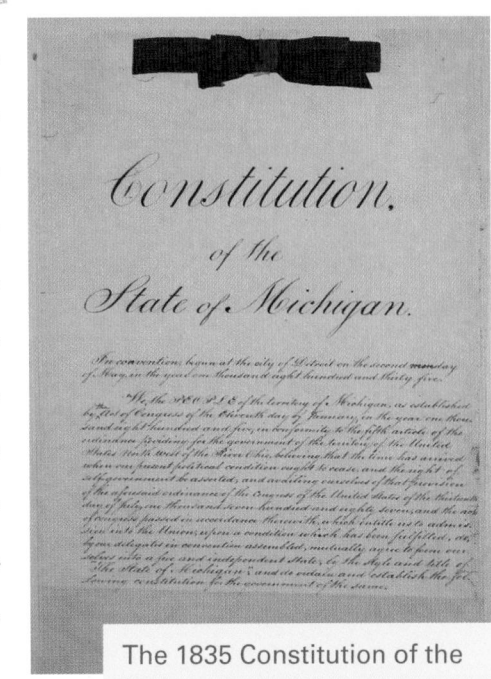

The 1835 Constitution of the State of Michigan is kept at the Michigan Library and Historical Center in Lansing.

Branches of Michigan's Government

Like the U.S. government, Michigan's government has three branches: executive, legislative, and judicial. Each branch has its own special functions. A system of checks and balances prevents any one branch from gaining too much power.

Executive Branch

The executive branch, headed by the governor, administers Michigan's laws. To be governor, a person must be at least thirty years old and have been a registered voter in the state for four years before the

The Reins of Power

When Antoine de la Mothe, Sieur de Cadillac, received permission in 1698 to establish Fort Pontchartrain, he was given complete power over the settlement. The control he enjoyed followed the centuries-old traditions of the power held by European nobles. He was both military commander and civilian ruler. He—and he alone—had authority to grant land to settlers. He could give or deny land to anyone he chose. Those who received land were required to give Cadillac a portion of whatever they raised on their land. He controlled all commerce and the mill that ground farmers' grain. He held a monopoly on the sale of gunpowder and alcohol. Fur trading could be conducted only by those who received licenses from him. Cadillac made up reasons to charge fees. He didn't give soldiers enough food. He ignored orders from French officials when they didn't suit him. He was, in short, a tyrant.

Perhaps it was experiences such as these that made recognition of the people's rights so important to Michiganders in the early 1800s. When they wrote the Michigan Constitution of 1835, they created a document that made clear that the people, not the government, held the reins of power. The very first statement in Article I declared, "All political power is inherent [fixed] in the people." It went on to state that the government existed solely for the benefit of the people, and no one man or group of men were entitled to special privileges that others did not enjoy. The constitution stated that people always have the right to change the government when the public good requires it. The constitution listed rights the people had that couldn't be taken from them, including freedom of religion, speech, and the press. The government couldn't subject people to unreasonable searches and seizures, nor could it deny trial by jury to those accused of crimes. The accused had the right to a speedy trial and a lawyer to represent them. The constitution gave the people the power to elect those who governed. It also gave them the power to propose amendments to the constitution.

gubernatorial election. The governor serves a four-year term and can serve for only two terms.

The governor's main office is in the George W. Romney Building in Lansing. There's an additional office in the state capitol, as well as offices in Detroit, Marquette, and Washington, D.C.

The state provides two homes for the governor. The executive residence in Lansing was built as a private home in 1957 and donated to the state in 1969. The governor also has a summer residence on Mackinac Island.

Elijah Myers designed the Michigan State Capitol, which was completed in 1879. The building was named a National Historic Landmark in 1992.

The governor's responsibilities include working with the legislature to create laws, signing or vetoing bills passed by the legislature, setting the state budget, and appointing people to government boards. The executive branch also includes the lieutenant governor, secretary of state, and state attorney general, who are elected by Michigan's voters, and a state treasurer, who is an unelected official appointed by the governor.

Legislative Branch

The legislative branch makes laws for the state. It's called the Michigan Legislature and is made up of two houses: the house of representatives and the senate. The house of representatives has 110 members who are elected for two-year terms. The senate has thirty-eight members who are elected to four-year terms.

In addition to making laws, the legislature levies taxes, helps the governor prepare the budget, and proposes amendments to the state constitution. The senate must approve the governor's appointments before they can take their positions.

The Hall of Justice, located in Lansing and completed in 2002, is home to the Michigan Supreme Court. The Hall of Justice also contains a museum.

Judicial Branch

The judicial branch interprets and enforces state laws. It has three levels of courts: trial courts, the Michigan Court of Appeals, and the Michigan Supreme Court. Trial courts include circuit courts (criminal and civil, or noncriminal, cases) and probate courts (cases involving young people). The Michigan Court of Appeals hears appeals from trial court judgments. Hearings are held before a panel of three court of appeals judges, and two of them must agree on the ruling. Judges for trial courts and the court of appeals are elected in nonpartisan elections for six-year terms. The Michigan Supreme

Court hears appeals from the court of appeals decisions. It can't hear all cases appealed to it, so it selects those with the broadest public importance. It's composed of seven justices who are elected in non-partisan elections for eight-year terms. The supreme court is also responsible for administrative supervision of all Michigan courts, which it does through the state court administrative office.

Local Governments

Michigan has eighty-three counties, each of which is run by a board of supervisors and also has a sheriff, county clerk, county treasurer, register of deeds, and prosecuting attorney. Some counties also have a county manager or administrator. Within counties, there are townships, which are run by a supervisor, clerk, treasurer, and up to four trustees. Within townships, there are cities, towns, and villages. Some are run by mayors, while others have councils that appoint a city manager. Local governments are responsible for such things as roads, parks, hospitals, public utilities, police, and fire protection. There are also special districts such as school districts. In addition to these local governments, each of Michigan's twelve federally recognized Native American tribes has its own government that rules tribal lands.

THE ECONOMY OF MICHIGAN

Michigan's economy was first based on natural resources. That changed in the late 1800s, when Michigan became a manufacturing state, with the automobile industry as the center of manufacturing. Soaring gasoline prices in 2008 and widespread economic troubles severely harmed the automobile industry and Michigan's economy as a whole. Yet even as the automobile industry struggled, there were bright spots in other parts of the state's economy. Michigan's gross domestic product (GDP) in 2008 was almost $382 billion. In February 2009, nearly four million people had jobs in the state.

Manufacturing in Michigan

By the late 1800s, Michigan was an industrial state, with shipbuilding and the manufacturing of cast-iron stoves among its principal industries. Its automobile industry began in 1899, when the Olds Motor Works factory was built in Detroit and began production the following year. Henry Ford, who founded the Ford Motor Company in 1903, revolutionized not only automobile manufacturing but all U.S. industry. In 1912, he introduced the assembly line, which greatly increased the speed of building a car, dramatically lowering prices and enabling many more people to buy automobiles. Ford also promoted

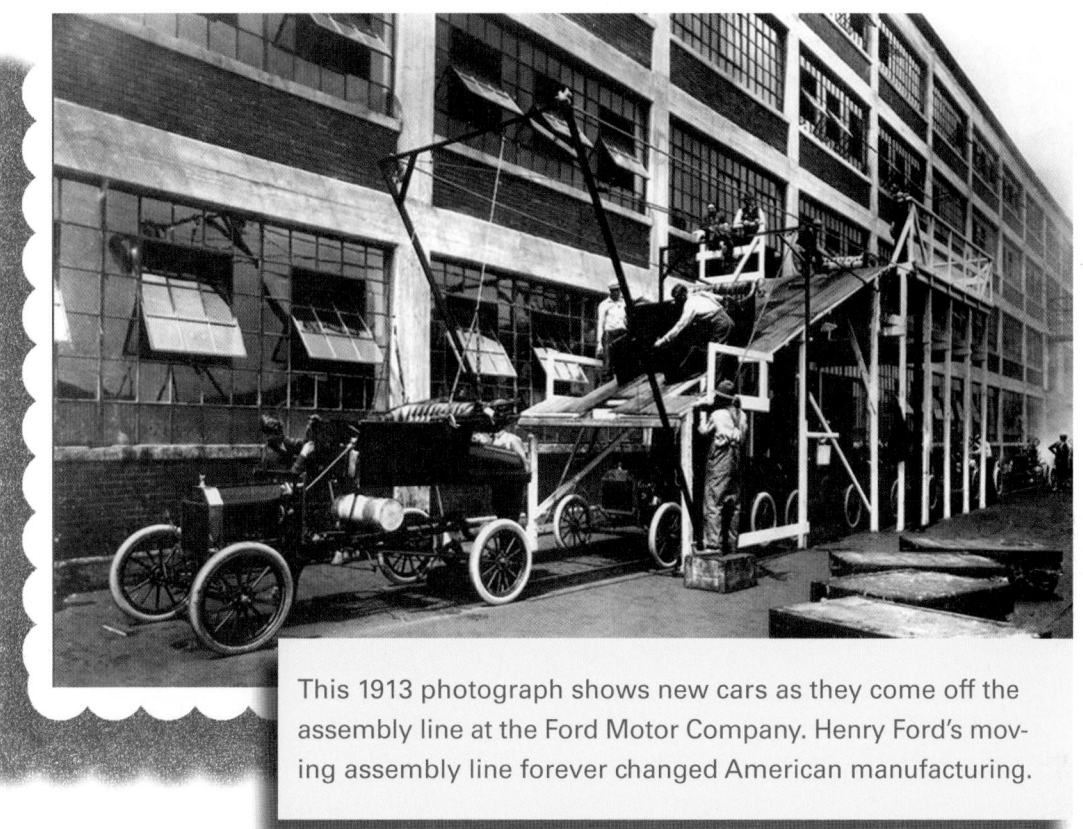

This 1913 photograph shows new cars as they come off the assembly line at the Ford Motor Company. Henry Ford's moving assembly line forever changed American manufacturing.

productivity by raising the minimum wage, shortening the workday, and granting workers a share in company profits.

In the late 1900s, imported Japanese cars attracted more and more buyers and began to challenge the dominance long enjoyed by American cars. In 2008, soaring gasoline prices and widespread economic problems led to a sharp drop in automobile sales. The major automobile manufacturers known as the Big Three—General Motors (GM), Chrysler, and Ford—faced serious monetary problems. GM and Chrysler were forced to seek financial aid from the U.S. government, lay off thousands of employees, and file for bankruptcy protection. This didn't mean that Chrysler and GM went out of

A Changing Economy

Michigan's economy has changed greatly over the centuries. The state's natural resources formed the foundation of its economy for hundreds of years. For early Native Americans, the region mostly offered good hunting, fishing, and a gathering place, although some also engaged in farming and trade. Many of the French who came in the 1600s were attracted by the possibility of growing wealthy from fur trading with Native Americans. When Cadillac founded Fort Pontchartrain, he hoped to build a farming community. That never happened. Farming is hard work, and most settlers who came were far more interested in the chance to get rich quickly from the fur trade.

In the 1800s, natural resources remained the basis of Michigan's economy, although the particular natural resources changed. In the mid-1800s, copper and iron mining, oil, and natural gas provided economic growth. Logging and farming dominated the economy in the late 1800s. Shipping on the Great Lakes also played a crucial role.

The foundation of the state's economy changed completely around 1900. Automobile manufacturing led the way, but it wasn't the only industry. Battle Creek became the nation's cereal capital. During the course of the twentieth century, many other kinds of manufacturing came to play important roles in Michigan's economy—metal products, machinery, computers, furniture (Grand Rapids was known as Furniture City), food products, chemicals, plastics, and rubber products. In the second half of the twentieth century, concerned by the economy's heavy dependence on the automobile industry, the governor promoted the development of agriculture and tourism.

Battered by the financial problems of 2008 and 2009, Michigan's economy suffered greatly. This forced Michiganders to launch a deeper, fuller exploration of economic alternatives that could return their state to a solid financial foundation and carry it into the future.

business; rather, it gave the companies financial protection while they tried to become more efficient and profitable. In spite of the Big Three's troubles, automobile manufacturing remains a main part of Michigan's economy.

For all the automobile industry's importance, Michigan's manufacturing is hardly limited to cars. Other important goods include fabricated metal products, machinery, food products, and plastic and rubber products. Some of the international companies that are headquartered in Michigan include Steelcase (office furniture), Dow Chemical Company (plastics and chemicals), Whirlpool Corporation (home appliances), Stryker (medical products and equipment), and La-Z-Boy (upholstered furniture).

Beyond Manufacturing: Other Aspects of Michigan's Economy

In spite of manufacturing's dominant role in Michigan's economy, it's hardly the state's only important economic enterprise. Agriculture and tourism are the two other primary sources of income and jobs. There are numerous other ventures that play smaller, yet vital, roles in Michigan's economy.

Agriculture

Even as Michigan's manufacturing struggled, the state's agriculture grew. Livestock and crop sales rose more than 50 percent between 2002 and 2007. In 2007, Michigan ranked first nationally in the production of three types of dry beans (black, cranberry, and small red), blueberries, tart cherries, and cucumbers for pickling. The state ranked

Traverse City's annual National Cherry Festival is a popular event in Michigan. These kids take part in the festival's cherry pie–eating contest.

seventh in sales of milk and other dairy products. Other important crops include wheat, oats, hay, corn, rye, potatoes, soybeans, sugar beets, apples, plums, grapes, carrots, and sweet cherries. Cattle, pigs, poultry, eggs, and wool from sheep are important, too.

With the growth of farming, however, have come problems. Most of the expansion has come from the increase in large livestock farms. These farms—sometimes called concentrated animal feeding operations (CAFOs) or factory farms—house thousands of animals in a single space. People living nearby often complain of pollution from the immense amounts of manure. Others have voiced concern about the treatment of the animals in such facilities. But to many in a state facing financial difficulties, any economic growth is welcome.

Tourism

Michigan is a popular destination for people who enjoy outdoor activities, such as hunting and fishing, winter sports, summer water sports, and hiking and camping. Even in the early 1900s, people came to northern Michigan to enjoy the summer resorts. The writer

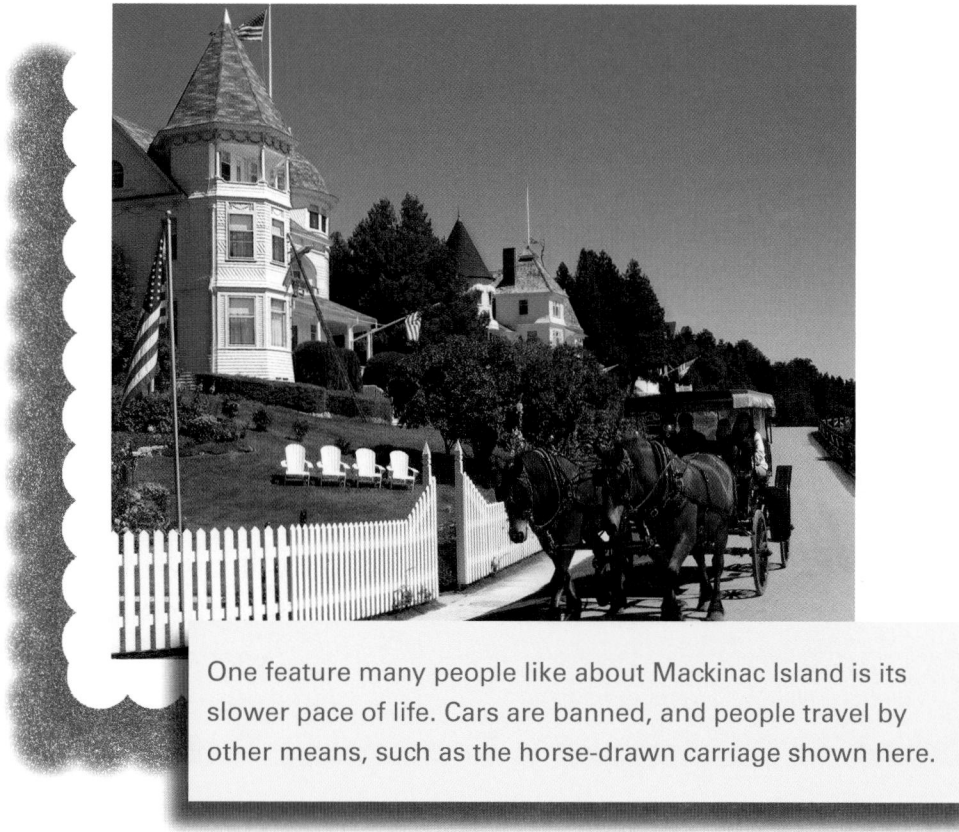

One feature many people like about Mackinac Island is its slower pace of life. Cars are banned, and people travel by other means, such as the horse-drawn carriage shown here.

Ernest Hemingway based many of his short stories on youthful summers spent at his family's cottage on Walloon Lake, near Petoskey.

Other people come to visit historic sites, such as Fort Michilimackinac, St. Ignace Mission (Father Jacques Marquette, who founded it in 1671, is buried there), and the Grand Hotel on Mackinac Island. Lighthouses lining the shores of Lake Superior attract lighthouse enthusiasts. The Henry Ford Museum and Greenfield Village (in Dearborn) allow visitors to explore many aspects of history. Many others visit the Soo Locks to admire the engineering accomplishment and watch ships pass through. For those who want something a bit different, there's the spring Tulip Festival in Holland, Michigan.

Hundreds of thousands of visitors come to see millions of tulips in bloom. The arts, spectator sports, and gambling also draw tourists to the state.

Still More Aspects of Michigan's Economy

Although manufacturing, agriculture, and tourism are the main pillars of Michigan's economy, there's more to it. Local, state, and federal governments provide more than 650,000 jobs. Michigan's vast forests furnish employment for loggers, forest and conservation workers, and their equipment suppliers. In April 2008, the Michigan Legislature passed a law designed to attract filmmakers to the state. By the year's end, filmmakers had spent more than $65 million in Michigan. This aspect of Michigan's economy is expected to grow in the future and have the added benefit of increasing tourism.

What Is Michigan's Economic Future?

No one knows for sure what the future holds, but it seems almost certain that the days of the automobile industry as it was during the twentieth century are over. New forms of transportation will be developed during the twenty-first century. Although Michigan may well play a part in that, it's not likely to be enough to restore the state's economy. Many people are working to chart a new economic path for Michigan. Governor Jennifer Granholm, who was elected Michigan's first female governor in 2002, and others have encouraged the development of renewable energy and a green economy. Some people are promoting what they call a "knowledge economy" to foster entrepreneurial activity and provide a highly educated, innovative labor force. In spite of the challenges faced by Michigan in the early twenty-first century, the future seems full of exciting possibilities.

Chapter 5

PEOPLE FROM MICHIGAN:
PAST AND PRESENT

Michigan has been home to many famous people in numerous fields of endeavor. They've influenced not only Michigan but also the nation. The following are some of the state's celebrated residents.

Cora Mae Brown (1914–1972) Brown and her family moved to Detroit from Alabama when she was eight. After being a social worker, police officer, and lawyer, she became the first African American woman elected to the Michigan State Senate in 1952. State senators chose her as their first African American female president one year later. Throughout her life, she fought the evils of racism and sexism.

Gerald R. Ford (1913–2006) Ford represented Michigan in Congress for twenty-five years. He became vice president of the United States in 1973 when President Richard Nixon chose him to replace Spiro Agnew, who had been forced to resign. Ford became president in 1974 when Nixon resigned. As president, Ford helped promote peace between Israel and Egypt. Grand Rapids, where he grew up, is home to the Gerald R. Ford Museum. The Ford Library is in Ann Arbor.

Henry Ford (1863–1947)

Born in what is today Dearborn, he founded the Ford Motor Company in 1903 and introduced the Model T in 1908. In 1913, he revolutionized the automobile industry with the introduction of the moving assembly line, which enabled him to greatly reduce the Model T's cost and make it affordable for the average family.

Daniel Frank Gerber (1873–1952)

Born in Fremont, he developed canned baby food in 1927 after his young daughter's doctor suggested straining foods for her.

Gerald Ford began his days early. This 1974 photo shows him on his way to his White House office at 7:15 AM.

Julie Harris (1925–)

One of the most celebrated actresses of the twentieth century, Harris, who was born and raised in Grosse Pointe, won five Tony Awards for her stage acting and three Emmy Awards for her television acting. She's also a member of the American Theatre Hall of Fame.

Derek Jeter (1974–)

Jeter was born in Pequannock, New Jersey, but grew up in Kalamazoo. He won national awards as a high school baseball player. The New York Yankees

This photograph captures Derek Jeter in action during a New York Yankees game. Jeter grew up in Kalamazoo and played baseball and basketball for Kalamazoo Central High School.

drafted him after he graduated in 1992. After playing in the minor leagues, he moved up to the Yankees in 1996 and helped them win four World Series titles. He won the American League Rookie of the Year Award in 1996. He became World Series Most Valuable Player in 2000 and captain of the Yankees in 2003. He won Gold Glove Awards in 2004, 2005, and 2006.

Michigan Singers

For many people, Detroit means music. In 1959, Barry Gordy Jr. founded the celebrated Motown Records (Motown, short for "motor town," is Detroit's nickname). But Michigan's famous singers aren't limited to Motown artists.

Madonna Louise Ciccone (1958–) Madonna was born in Bay City. She's released more than a dozen albums and acted in numerous films.

Smokey Robinson (1940–) Born in Detroit, Robinson had dozens of hits as a member of the 1960s Motown group the Miracles and as a solo artist.

Diana Ross (1944–) She achieved fame as the lead singer of the Motown group the Supremes. As a solo artist, she was the first woman to have six number 1 songs.

Bob Seger (1945–) This rock singer began his career in Detroit in 1961. Two 1976 albums—*Live Bullet* and *Night Moves*—brought him national fame.

Stevie Wonder (1950–) Born in Saginaw, Wonder began recording for Motown when he was only twelve. He was inducted into the Rock and Roll Hall of Fame in 1989.

Diana Ross *(center)* appears with the Supremes in this 1964 photo.

Donald B. Keck (1941–) Keck was born in Lansing and attended Michigan State University, where he received a Ph.D. in physics in 1967. In 1968, he was hired by Corning Glass Works, where he worked with Robert Maurer and Peter Schultz to develop practical, efficient fiber optics. The three men received the National Medal of Technology in 2000 for their work. Keck retired from Corning in 2002.

William Keith Kellogg (1860–1951) With his brother, John Harvey, he developed cereal and promoted it as a healthy breakfast food. In 1906, he established the Battle Creek Toasted Corn Flakes Company, which later became the Kellogg Company. Kellogg believed in giving back to society and gave millions of dollars to charitable causes.

Ryan Miller (1980–) As goaltender for the hockey team of Michigan State University in East Lansing, where he was born, he won numerous awards. He's been goaltender for the Buffalo (New York) Sabres since 2002 and is considered one of the best goaltenders in the National Hockey League.

Chief Okemos (about 1775–1858) He was an honored and respected Chippewa chief. Because of his bravery in battle, he became a chief when he was only twenty. By 1814, he had grown tired of fighting and signed a peace treaty with the U.S. government.

Harriet Quimby (1875–1912) Born near Coldwater, she became a newspaper writer, editor, and prize-winning photographer. However, she's most famous as the first

In 1911, Harriet Quimby posed in the cockpit of her plane. That same year, Quimby became the first woman to fly at night and to fly over Mexico.

woman to get a pilot's license in the United States (1911). In 1912, Quimby became the first woman to fly across the English Channel.

Shavehead (early 1800s) The exact dates of this Potawatomi chief's birth and death aren't known. White settlers called him Shavehead because, like many of his ancestors, he shaved most of his head. Both whites and Native Americans feared him as a fierce warrior.

Chris Van Allsburg (1949–) He's an artist who began his career as a sculptor but wound up as a writer and illustrator of children's books. His first book, *The Garden of Abdul Gasazi*, was published in 1979. He's perhaps most famous for the award-winning books *Jumanji* and *The Polar Express*, both of which were made into movies. He's also received the Regina Medal for lifetime achievement in children's literature.

Timeline

9500 BCE	Ancestors of Native Americans arrive.
1622	French explorer Étienne Brûlé becomes the first European to see Michigan.
1668	Father Jacques Marquette founds the first permanent European settlement in Michigan at Sault Ste. Marie.
1701	Antoine Cadillac founds settlement that becomes Detroit.
1763	The great Ottawa chief Pontiac tries to take over Detroit but fails. The British take over Michigan.
1783	The newly formed United States of America takes over Michigan.
1805	Congress establishes the Territory of Michigan.
1835	Michigan prepares for statehood by writing its first constitution.
1837	Michigan becomes the twenty-sixth state.
1840s	Copper and iron mining begin in the U.P.
1861–1865	Michigan sides with the Union during the American Civil War.
1899	Ransom E. Olds sets up the Olds Motor Works in Detroit.
1903	Henry Ford establishes the Ford Motor Company.
1908	Ford's hugely successful Model T first appears.
1935	The United Automobile Workers Union is established in Michigan.
1963	Michigan's new constitution is written.
1974	Gerald R. Ford, who grew up in Grand Rapids, becomes president.
1987	The Women's Historical Center and Hall of Fame opens in Lansing.
2002	Jennifer Granholm becomes Michigan's first female governor.
2008	Michigan Legislature passes the Michigan Film Production Credit program to attract filmmakers to Michigan.
2009	Governor Granholm proposes to make Michigan a leader in green energy production.

Michigan at a Glance

State motto	*Si quaeris peninsulam amoenam circumspice* (If you seek a pleasant peninsula, look about you.)
State capital	Lansing
State seal	The coat of arms with the words "The Great Seal of the State of Michigan."
State flower	Apple blossom
State bird	Robin
State tree	White pine
State flower	Dwarf lake iris
Statehood date and number	January 26, 1837; the twenty-sixth state
State nicknames	The Great Lakes State, the Wolverine State
Total area and U.S. rank	96,716 square miles (250,494 sq km); eleventh-largest state
Population	9,938,000
Highest elevation	Mount Avron, which is 1,979 feet (603 m) above sea level
Lowest elevation	Along Lake Erie, which is 571 feet (174 m) above sea level

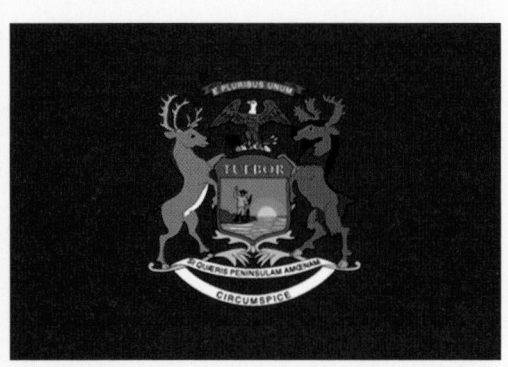

State Flag

State Seal

Major rivers	Menominee River, Muskegon River, Grand River, Kalamazoo River, Saginaw River
Major lakes	Lake St. Clair; Lakes Michigan, Superior, Huron, Erie
Hottest temperature recorded	112°F (44°C) on July 13, 1936, at Mio
Coldest temperature recorded	51°F (–46°C) on February 9, 1934, at Vanderbilt
Origin of state name	From the Chippewa (Ojibwa) word *michigama*, meaning "large lake"
Chief agricultural products	Apples, cherries, beef cattle, blueberries, corn, greenhouse and nursery plants, hogs, milk, soybeans, wheat
Major industries	Food; metal, plastic, and rubber products; machinery; transportation equipment; mining (iron ore, copper, natural gas, oil, portland cement)

Robin

Apple blossom

GLOSSARY

assembly line An arrangement of machines, equipment, and workers in which the product passes from worker to worker along the line until assembly is complete.

bedrock A layer of solid rock below soil.

cast iron A form of iron mixed with carbon and other elements that is often used in building and for stoves.

constitution A written document that sets up the principles and laws for a state or country's government.

ecosystem A community of plants, animals, and their environment functioning as a single unit.

entrepreneurial Having to do with business.

Great Lakes The chain of five lakes: Superior, Michigan, Huron, Erie, and Ontario.

gross domestic product (GDP) The total value of all goods and services produced in a state or country.

gubernatorial Relating to a state governor or the office of a state governor.

immigration The movement of people from one country into a new country with plans to stay in the new country.

inducted Admitted as a member.

innovative Introducing new ideas, methods, or devices.

lake effect Caused when cold, dry air passing over a lake mixes with warm, moist air rising from the lake, resulting in precipitation.

peccary A large wild animal related to pigs but covered with stiff, grayish hair.

petition A formal written request to an official or government body.

precipitation Any form of moisture that falls from the sky, including rain and snow.

sediment Matter deposited by glaciers, wind, or water.

suspension bridge A bridge that suspends the roadway from cables.

trustees People who are responsible for supervising a territory.

veto To refuse to approve a legislative bill, thus preventing it from becoming law.

wetlands Areas of land that are covered with shallow water or have soil full of water, such as marshes, swamps, and bogs.

wolverine A very large, strong member of the weasel family.

Historical Society of Michigan

1305 Abbot Road

East Lansing, MI 48823

(517) 324-1828

Web site: http://www.hsmichigan.org

Established in 1828, the society's mission is to foster a deeper understanding of and appreciation for Michigan history through programs and publications.

Michigan Library and Historical Center

702 West Kalamazoo Street

Lansing, MI 48915

(517) 373-3559

Web site: http://www.michigan.gov/museum

The Michigan Historical Museum offers five levels of permanent and changing exhibits that tell the story of Michigan's past up to the late twentieth century.

Michigan Lighthouse Conservancy

P.O. Box 973

Fenton, MI 48430

(810) 750-9236

Web site: http://www.michiganlights.com

The Michigan Lighthouse Conservancy is devoted to promoting the preservation of the state's lighthouses, lifesaving station structures, and the objects associated with them.

Michigan Maritime Museum

260 Dyckman Road

South Haven, MI 49090

(269) 637-8078 or (800) 747-3810

Web site: http://michiganmaritimemuseum.org

The museum is dedicated to the preservation of Michigan's Great Lakes and waterways history and culture.

Michigan Nature Association

326 East Grand River Avenue

Williamston, MI 48895

(517) 655-5655

Web site: http://www.michigannature.org

Founded in 1952, the association acquires, protects, and maintains natural habitats for endangered species and hosts a program of natural history study and conservation education.

Michigan Wildlife Conservancy

6380 Drumheller Road

P.O. Box 393

Bath, MI 48808

(517) 641-7677

Web site: http://miwildlife.org

The conservancy was founded in 1982 to provide technical and financial aid for landowners and managers to restore and maintain wildlife habitat on their land.

Michigan Women's Historical Center and Hall of Fame

213 West Main Street

Lansing, MI 48933

(517) 484-1880

Web site: http://www.michiganwomenshalloffame.org

Opened in 1987, the Michigan Women's Historical Center and Hall of Fame displays cultural and historical exhibits on the accomplishments and achievements of Michigan women.

Web Sites

Due to the changing nature of Internet links, Rosen Publishing has developed an online list of Web sites related to the subject of this book. This site is updated regularly. Please use this link to access the list:

http://www.rosenlinks.com/uspp/mipp

Arrathoon, Leigh A. *Summer of the Bear: An Historical Novel About the Anishinabeg and the Fur Traders in Michigan*. Rochester, MI: Paint Creek Press, 2005.

Burcar, Colleen, with Gene Taylor. *Michigan Curiosities: Quirky Characters, Roadside Oddities & Other Offbeat Stuff*. 2nd ed. Guilford, CT: Globe Pequot Press, 2007.

Burns, Virginia Law. *Bold Women in Michigan History*. Missoula, MT: Mountain Press Publishing Co., 2006.

Cochrane, Timothy. *Minong—The Good Place: Ojibwe and Isle Royale*. East Lansing, MI: Michigan State University Press, 2009.

Domm, Robert W. *Michigan: Yesterday & Today*. Osceola, WI: Voyageur Press, 2009.

Erdrich, Louise. *The Porcupine Year*. New York, NY: HarperCollins, 2008.

Faber, Don. *The Toledo War: The First Michigan-Ohio Rivalry*. Ann Arbor, MI: The University of Michigan Press, 2008.

Gallagher, John. *Great Architecture of Michigan*. Detroit, MI: Wayne State University Press, 2008.

Godfrey, Linda S. *Weird Michigan: Your Travel Guide to Michigan's Local Legends and Best Kept Secrets*. New York, NY: Sterling Publishing Co., Inc., 2006.

Johnson, Elizabeth M. *Michigan* (From Sea to Shining Sea). New York, NY: Scholastic Children's Press, 2009.

Kchodl, Joseph J. *The Complete Guide to Michigan Fossils*. Ann Arbor, MI: The University of Michigan Press, and Traverse City, MI: Petoskey Publishing Co., 2006.

Knott, John, ed. *Michigan: Our Land, Our Water, Our Heritage*. Ann Arbor, MI: The University of Michigan Press, published in cooperation with the Nature Conservancy, 2008.

Lehto, Steve. *Michigan's Columbus: The Life of Douglass Houghton*. Royal Oak, MI: Momentum Books, 2009.

May, George S., and JoEllen Vinyard. *Michigan, the Great Lakes State: An Illustrated History*. Sun Valley, CA: American Historical Press, 2005.

O'Connor, Ryan, Michael A. Kost, and Joshua G. Cohen. *Prairies and Savannas in Michigan: Rediscovering Our Natural Heritage*. East Lansing, MI: Michigan State University Press, 2009.

Porter, Adele. *Wild About Michigan Birds: A Youth's Guide to the Birds of Michigan*. Cambridge, MN: Adventure Publications, Inc., 2009.

Powers, Tom. *Michigan State and National Parks: A Complete Guide*. 4th ed. Chicago, IL: Thunder Bay Press, 2007.

BIBLIOGRAPHY

History Detroit. "History Detroit: 1701–2001." HistoryDetroit.com. Retrieved April 12, 2009 (http://www.historydetroit.com).

Holman, J. Alan, and Margaret B. Holman. *The Michigan Roadside Naturalist*. Ann Arbor, MI: The University of Michigan Press, 2006.

Ivacko, Thomas. "Michigan's Economic Transition: Toward a Knowledge Economy." University of Michigan Center for Local, State, and Urban Policy, Policy Report 9: Summer 2007.

Mackinac Bridge Authority. "Facts & Figures." Retrieved April 15, 2009 (http://www.mackinacbridge.org/facts--figures-16).

Michigan Constitutional Convention. "Constitution of Michigan of 1835." Detroit, MI: 1835.

Michigan Constitutional Convention. "Constitution of the State of Michigan of 1963." Lansing, MI: 1962.

Michigan Department of Energy, Labor & Economic Growth, Bureau of Labor Market Information & Strategic Initiatives. "Labor Market Information: Current Employment Statistics, Unadjusted Data, February 2009." Milmi.org. Retrieved April 13, 2009 (http://www.milmi.org/admin/uploadedPublications/940_micaetmm.htm).

Michigan Department of Natural Resources. "Lake Basins & Ecoregions." Michigan.gov. Retrieved April 8, 2009 (http://www.michigan.gov/dnr/0,1607,7-153-10370_30909_31053---,00.html).

Michigan Oil & Gas Producers Education Foundation. *Michigan Oil & Gas Facts 2008*. Lansing, MI: Michigan Oil & Gas Producers Education Foundation, 2008.

Rubenstein, Bruce A., and Lawrence E. Ziewacz. *Michigan: A History of the Great Lakes State*. 4th ed. Wheeling, IL: Harlan Davidson, Inc., 2008.

Runk, David. "First Michigan Wolverine Spotted in 200 Years." MSNBC.com. Retrieved April 16, 2009 (http://www.msnbc.msn.com/id/4374309).

Sault Ste. Marie Convention & Visitors Bureau. "Our Local History." Saultstemarie.com. Retrieved April 12, 2009 (http://www.saultstemarie.com/our-local-history-9).

Schaetzl, Randall J. "Climate: Patterns of Weather and Climate in Michigan." Earthscape.org. Retrieved April 8, 2009 (http://www.earthscape.org/t2/scr01/scr01hc.html).

U.S. Census Bureau. "Michigan—Place and County Subdivision." Census.gov. Retrieved April 12, 2009 (http://factfinder.census.gov/servlet/GCTTable?_bm = y&-geo_id = 04000US26&-_box_head_nbr = GCT-PH1-R&-ds_name = DEC_2000_SF1_U&-_lang = en&-format = ST-7S&-_sse = on).

INDEX

About the Author

Janey Levy, the author of more than one hundred books for young readers of all ages, is an editor and writer who lives in Colden, New York. She had the pleasure of living and teaching in southern Michigan for two years and has also visited the state's famously beautiful Upper Peninsula.

Photo credits:

Cover (top) pp. 1, 3, 6, 8, 11, 12, 18, 21, 22, 24, 25, 31, 38, 40 Wikipedia; cover (bottom) Kerry Kelly/NPS; p. 4 © GeoAtlas; p. 7 © www.istockphoto.com/Yan-chun Tung; p. 9 © Keto Gyekis/Shutterpoint; p. 13 Wisconsin Historical Society; p. 14 U.S. Army Corps of Engineers; p. 15 Mackinac Island State Park Commission; pp. 17, 28 © AP Images; p. 19 Courtesy Archives of Michigan; p. 29 Shutterstock.com; p. 32 Dirk Halstead/Time & Life Pictures/Getty Images; p. 33 Scott Boehm/Getty Images; p. 34 RB/Redferns/Getty Images; p. 36 Library of Congress Prints and Photographs Division; p. 39 Courtesy of Robesus, Inc.

Designer: Les Kanturek; Editor: Kathy Kuhtz Campbell;
Photo Researcher: Amy Feinberg